9/26/72

From
Charlotte

It Could Be Verse

amazon.com

GREETINGS FROM AMAZON.COM

We are pleased to have located this out of print book for your personal library. You may note some remnants of your book's past life—an autograph, a dog-eared corner, some yellowed pages. We guarantee that it will be, at the very least, in good reading condition. If this book does not meet your expectations, please take advantage of our enclosed return policy (found on the back of the order invoice).

Amazon.com has reunited thousands of book lovers with the out of print titles they thought they'd never see again. We hope you enjoy your book, and we look forward to scouring more dusty shelves for your next out of print selection.

Thank you for shopping with us!

Please send your comments to:
feedback@amazon.com

amazon.com
Books, Music and More
http://www.amazon.com

It Could Be Verse

Victor Buono

Nash Publishing, Los Angeles

Library of Congress Catalog Card Number: 72-81829
Standard Book Number: 8402-1276-3

Published simultaneously in the United States and Canada
by Nash Publishing Corporation, 9255 Sunset Boulevard,
Los Angeles, California 90069.

Printed in the United States of America.

First Printing.

Contents

It
Could
Be
Verse

Do You Have It in a 60 Extra-long?

I have grown both weak and weary
Of the silly modern theory·
That in order to be known as chic,
One must not look well fed.
According to the magazines
If one cannot wear tapered jeans
One might as well wear saddle bags
'Cause socially you're dead.

Now, just because some lazy gland
Has gotten somewhat out of hand
And caused me to expand
Into the shape in which you find me,
I see no cause to hide my face,
I've got my share of manly grace
It just got wadded in one place
And some got stuck behind me.

To me it's inconceivable
That one could find believable
The thought that one must have a shape
Exactly like his chum.
I simply won't apologize
For being of a grander size —

When everyone's a seedless grape
It's great to be a plum.

And if the girls refuse to dig me
Just because I'm not a pygmy,
Then I try to make them see my view
That beauty comes in barrels, too;
And precious gemstones grow in clumps
And treasures can be found in dumps
And silver hides in heaps.
To heck with all your fashion trends,
I'd rather be myself, my friends,
I love to be a limousine when all the rest are jeeps. ◆

Let's Hear It for Mrs. Sprat

Ever since the day I learned
That *Fat*'s a title to be earned,
I've tried and vied and burned and yearned
To be called simply that.

You might think it etiquette
To say that I am heavy set,
Or just big-boned. Ya wanna bet?
I'm fat! I'm fat! I'm fat!

Portly, chubby, plump and stout,
No one wants to be a lout —
But why not let it all hang out
And go ahead and call me fat?

Please don't think you're being kind
By pretending to be blind;
Just take a look at my—physique:
The only word is "fat." ◆

Lard Lib

Paradise was very nice
For Adam and his Madam,
Until they filched the fruit and took the fall —
We lost our place and fell from grace
And you can bet we can't forget
That eating is the oldest sin of all.

Since Man first fell they've made life hell
For folks who tend to make things bend,
And I for one, or two, can take no more:
I sound the call for fat folk all
To follow me to liberty;
I hold the lamp beside the kitchen door.

Too long have we been forced to be
The slapsticks of society;
Too long have we drunk Tab while they drink wine.
Our cause may seem a hopeless dream
But faith and pride are on our side;
Our acids may be fatty but we're fine.

The time is now and we must vow
To find a place within our race,

And sound our horns and let our banners flutter,
Bein' thin is where it's been
But bein' fat is where it's at —
Forward, fellow fatties! Pass the butter! ◆

Strange New World

Someday when I'm skinny
And can tie my shoes with ease,
I'll contemplate the strange new world
That lies below my knees.

I'll eat Danish pastry with no sense of guilt,
My seams will stay sewn and my collars won't wilt,
I'll hop aboard airplanes and not have to mention
My need for an eighteen-inch seat belt extension.

I'll swim in the ocean—I can't, now, you see,
'Cause I'm always attacked by a boatload of kooks
Yelling "Ahab was right! He's as white as can be!"
As they hurl their harpoons at my flukes.

Or I may work it out so my body gets thin
While my head becomes terribly fat,
I could certainly be vice president then
(And I hope he can't sue me for that).

I'll pass groups of kids and delight in their playing
And not have to pretend I can't hear what they're saying,
I'll jump in a bathtub that's filled to the top
And not have to fear that the water will slop.

I'm too big for most bathtubs, you see,
There's just enough room, if I'm lucky,

For a half pint of water, and me,
But no room for soap, or my ducky.

I'll get me some sneakers and go in for sports:
Skydiving, polo and hockey!
I'll dazzle the gridirons, diamonds and courts,
Acrobat, goalie and jockey.

I could be a jockey right now,
But my horse would be needing a truss,
And you can't get good odds if you're riding a cow,
And how does one saddle a bus?

I'll have a series on Channel One
"Metrecal brings you: The Flying Bun!"
I'll win golden medals and trophies of bronze
For skiing and driving a car at Le Mans.

Racing cars are out for people who are stout,
I'm too big to make the Maserati scene,
To fit me in a Fiat is impossible without
A shoehorn and a case of Vaseline.

Yeah, someday I'll be skinny and I'll have a lot of fun,

I'll live on cyclamates and cottage cheese,
But now I see the waiter has my baked Alaska done:
"Set it here, and fetch another if you please." ◆

Moby
Vic

Any guy who thinks that he
Can diet on a ship at sea
Will soon perceive the nonsense of this notion.
I know I cannot forget
The moment that my ship first set
Its course across the North Atlantic Ocean. . .

I should have known I had no chance
Of slimming down en route to France,
But now I know how hopeless was my hope:
The odds I'd ever see my toes
Weren't anywhere as good as those
That Jessel has of being voted Pope.

For as we sailed I chanced to hear
A weak voice calling from the pier,
"Victor! Bon voyage! Don't eat too much!"
Then I saw this gnomish fellow
With a face of greening yellow
Like a scrawny Rumpelstiltskin on a crutch.

The sickly runt's identity
Didn't really dawn on me
Till we were far at sea; then came the shock.
I stood there pale and paralyzed

As suddenly I realized
I'd left my self-control back on the dock.

There I was upon the sea,
Fourteen tons of food and me,
And seven days to get it all inside me;
Master chefs and salty air
And butter, butter everywhere,
And not a jot of discipline to guide me.

Lobster stuffed with duck and goose,
Potted penguin, scrambled moose,
French-fried eagles, truffles by the bunch,
A school of fish, a flock of lamb,
A grove of fruit, a herd of ham,
And that takes care of breakfast, now for brunch.

From dawn to dusk I stuffed myself
With peacock ears and pickled elf
And walrus eggs (both real and imitation);
Four days out they said that I
Had so reduced the food supply
That A and B decks perished of starvation.

And once I caused an awful row
By going forward to the bow

To nibble on a bit of candied otter;
I realized my blunder
As the prow went six feet under
And the screws were spinning free above the water.

It wasn't very long before
A note came from the Commodore
Inviting me to join him for a drink;
He said, "This might sound rude I fear,
But would you care to volunteer
To double as a lifeboat if we sink?

"And if and when you might decide
To promenade the starboard side,
I'd like a little warning of some sort.
Just give me half an hour in which
My crew will have a chance to switch
The cargo and the passengers to port.

"And considering the weight you've gained
Our gangplank might be overstrained,
So when we land, please, help with one thing more —
We'll lower you in a plastic sack
And when you're floating on your back
The pastry chef will straddle you and paddle you ashore."

So if you wish to correlate
An ocean trip with losing weight,
Or fitting in a smaller pair of pants,
You're more than welcome to try it;
But I can vouch that a sea-going diet
Cannot hope to stand the chance
   That General Lee would have stood,
   Upon losing his sword and asking to borrow
     General Grant's,
   Or General Grant would have stood,
   Upon losing his sword and asking to borrow
     General Lee's,
   Or I have of winning the Pulitzer Prize in poetry
   For crumby little rhymes such as these.◆

To
My Muse

When flowers doze upon their loamy beds,
And oaken sentries nod their noble heads,
Any piny cushions snug the cuddled fawns,
And dewy gems bejewel the dreaming lawns,
I sit and wait in patience born of pain
For some sweet sonnet to ignore my brain.

And as aurora lifts her rosy veil,
My muse approaches — haggard, had, and pale,
Fetid, fingered, rancid, rank and frowsy
No wonder all my poetry's so lousy. ◆

Bird
Song

Some men call the girl they love
Their chickadee or turtledove
And other such foul names I find revolting.
The things that names like these suggest
Dine on bugs and live in nests
And scratch for worms, when they're not busy
   moulting.

And pussycats and bunnyrabbits
Have distressing social habits;
Lambs and ducks are sweet, but spoil the lawn.
But I'm not one to criticize
'Cause lovers see through filtered eyes:
If they dig pink eyes, fangs and fleas, right on!

My sweetheart's not at all like all the rest,
She's much more like the things I like best.

She's my brisket of beauty, my pretty pink parfait,
My tenderloin of tenderness, my passionate pâté.
My canapé, café au lait,
My crown rib roast so regal,
My barbeque, and fondue too,
My hash, the kind that's legal.

My sweetheart's not at all like all the rest,
She's much more like the things I like best.

Her mouth is like a cherry, small and sweet,
Her cheeks are apples, firm and fresh and red,
In her complexion cream and peaches meet.
My tootsie has a tutti-frutti head,

She's as peaceful as a pickle
And as rich as pumpernickel
And as happy as salami;
She's my hot pastrami mommy
Heaven sent me as her lover
'Cause there's just so darn much of her
She's my manna à la mode sent from above
Together we're an automat of love.

My sweetheart's not at all like the rest,
She's exactly like the things I like the best. ◆

New Gig

As heaven's portals opened wide
A brand new saint came marchin' in;
For one who recently had died
He wore a most aggressive grin.

They handed him a golden horn,
Just polished by a cherub's wing,
A gift from friends long since reborn:
Parker and Handy and Bix and King.

He mopped his forehead with a cloud,
Then blew a riff so rich and rare
That Gabriel arose and bowed
And moved to second chair.

He strode straight into paradise
As lofts of angels flowered in song:
"Hello, Satchmo, it's so nice
To have you back where you belong." ◆

Bless Me, Doctor

Bless me, doctor, I have sinned
Since seeing you last week,
The Spirit had the will to win
But, oh, the Flesh was weak.

You warned me that I must deprive
My appetites, and somehow strive
To conquer these compulsive drives
To eat which now obsess me.
You told me all the foods to ban
You gave me pills to aid the plan
I still outweigh my own sedan
And so I must confess me.

On Monday, I awoke at eight
Determined to reduce my weight,
Dry toast and tea is all I ate
Then Satan came to test me.
The pills had made me feel so great
I felt I ought to celebrate
I made French toast and licked the plate
Bless me, doctor, bless me.

On Tuesday as I lay in bed
I still had sixty pounds to shed,

But thoughts of cheesecake filled my head
And started to enslave me.
"The Devil can't trick me," I said,
"I want some cheesecake, but instead
I'll eat two loaves of diet bread!"
Save me, doctor, save me.

On Wednesday I went quite insane:
At eight I switched on Jack LaLanne,
By nine I was a knot of pain
And Satan came to snare me.
By ten I couldn't stand the strain,
I dialed a famous chicken chain,
"Send two with malts and three more plain!"
Spare me, Colonel, spare me.

But Thursday brought the worst disgrace:
On Thursday I was very base;
I looked the Devil in the face —
I should have known he'd trap me.
I got into a kind of race
Which I soon won with easy grace.
The race was in a pizza place —
Slap me, someone, slap me.

And now it's Friday and I'm back,

A saturated cul de sac,
A hopeless munchomaniac,
But nothing can suppress me.
So put some fresh pills in my sack,
I'm ready for the fiend's attack;
But while I wait I'll have a snack —
Pass the bread, and bless me. ◆

Guilty

Some men can sin and conceal it,
They're bandits, but no one gets wise;
When I sin, my seams will reveal it,
My crimes are proclaimed by my size.

Some folks are awful unlawful,
They're loaded with loot but who'd know it?
I try to sneak in a waffle
And five minutes later I show it.

Since pounds are like crimes they can nail me
On well over three hundred counts,
And try me for each pound and jail me —
I hope I'm not fined by the ounce.

I'm guilty of imperfect diet,
My shape shows I'm pizza-pie prone;
I know it's no good to deny it —
Now, who wants to cast the first stone? ◆

Oh Tempora!
Oh Calcutta!

The art we call acting is awfully exacting.
An actor cannot avoid pain;
He needn't be smart but he's gotta have art,
And it helps if he's slightly insane.

The great ones are gone: Ethel, Lionel, John,
And Lorre (the sinister elf);
We've lost Laughton and Wynn and Greenstreet and Flynn,
And I don't feel too well myself.

But the current desire for scanty attire
Leaves actors like me in a daze,
To be poised and composed with one's bottom exposed
Ain't required in classical plays.

There are movies and plays being offered these days
Which look, smell and sound much the same
As a basketball team snapping towels in the steam
In the locker room after a game.

The language is crude, the characters nude,
Their actions I can't bear to mention.
The emotions are raw as the ones that we saw
At the last Democratic convention.

So don't bother gaining professional training

And don't even bother rehearsing,
Be a star overnight and the critics' delight:
Just take off your pants and start cursing. ◆

He Looks
So Natural

Here he lies who made our lives a hell,
Still so stiff and waxen and disdainful;
He hated us and yet we wish him well —
We only wish his death had been more painful.

He passed in the quintessence of contentment,
With fluffy pillows, priests, and scented tallows.
So pardon our residual resentment,
'Cause pricks like him should cash out on the gallows.

Why is he within this coffin?
He pushed his luck just once too often!
The rites are completed and so we depart
With a smile on our lips and a stake in his heart. ◆

Afterthought

His life was like a modern play
No star, no plot.
We buried him at dawn today;
So far. . . so what? ◆

Rome
Pome

Rome eternal, high and palmy,
Home of Caesar and salami,
   Sunwashed city, peaceful, holy,
   Full of art and ravioli.
Buy a treasure rich and strange,
Count your blessings, count your change.
   Marble fountains filled with coins
   By hopeful spinsters from Des Moines.
See the lovers: a bankrupt duke
And a bulging widow from Dubuque;
She loves his blue eyes, his white hair,
He loves her blue-white solitaire;
   A starving painter, a lonely matron,
   She needs a paint job, he a patron.
Piazza Navona, Piazza d'Espagna,
Viva Bernini, viva lasagna.
   A marble Venus veiled in dust
   With a chopped-off chin and a busted bust;
Mighty Mars the god of battle,
His nose is a paperweight now in Seattle.
   Power fades and glory tumbles;
   Atsadaway the pizza crumbles.◆

Suffer
the
Children

Christmas being nearly nigh,
I went into a store to buy
Some toys to give away on Christmas Day.
If what I saw upon the shelves
Was made by Santa and his elves,
Then Santa must have joined the N.R.A.

Santa Claus must be a Hawk;
The toys he gives kids are a shock—
A rifle for Tom and a pistol for Ted.
Oh come all ye faithful . . . bang bang, you're dead!
No doubt he's had bombsights installed in his sled.
He once was a dove, but, alas,
He now must think war is a gas.

Something's come over Saint Nick;
All of a sudden, he's sick:
Why else would he try to pervert and destroy
Bethlehem's tidings of comfort and joy
By giving a child a violent toy?
A baby was born, but which one:
Christ? Or Attila the Hun?

Santa's just hung up on war,
He must think the Peace Corps's a bore,
A search of the pack on his back will reveal

Intricate weapons of plastic and steel,
They're phony, of course, but their meaning is real;
Consider the thought they instill,
Playtime means . . . learning to kill.♦

A
Fat Man's
Prayer

Lord my soul is ripped with riot
Incited by my wicked diet;
"We are what we eat" said a wise old man,
And Lord if that's true, I'm a garbage can.

To rise on Judgment Day it's plain
That at my weight I'll need a crane,
So grant me strength that I may not fall
Into the clutches of cholesterol.

May my flesh with carrot curls be sated
That my soul may be polyunsaturated,
And show me the light that I may bear witness
To the president's council on physical fitness.

At oleomargarine I'll never mutter,
For the road to hell is spread with butter,
And cream is cursed and cake is awful,
And Satan is hiding in every waffle.

Mephistopheles lurks in provolone,
The Devil is in each slice of bologna,
Beelzebub is a chocolate drop
And Lucifer is a lollipop.

Give me this day my daily slice
But cut it thin and toast it twice;

I beg upon my dimpled knees:
Deliver me from jujubes.

And when my days of trial are done
And my war with malted milk is won,
Let me stand with the saints in heaven
In a shining robe, size thirty-seven.

I can do it, Lord, if you'll show to me
The virtues of lettuce and celery,
If you'll teach me the evil of mayonnaise,
The sinfulness of Hollandaise,
And pasta à la Milanaise
Potatoes à la Lyonnaise
And crisp-fried chicken from the South;
Lord, if you love me, shut my mouth.◆

Miscellanea

Although my belt may not be svelte
I've never felt disgusted;
The kind of pot that I have got
Will never get me busted.◆

Continental chambermaids are very hard to shock
They wait until you're naked, then they enter,
  then they knock.◆

Hope is a thing with feathers perched in the soul all day:
It does its little business, and then it flies away.◆

I guide my life as I do my diet:
It's nuts to knock it before you try it.◆

Life's a stage, the poets prate,
A movie melodrama;
And some of us are super-8
And some are cinerama.◆

To the poor man I offer a simple solution
To ease his troubled mind:
Step to the rear of the Constitution
And quit while you're behind.◆

Once I turned a somersault
Quite near the San Andreas fault.
Later as I nursed my knee,
A telegram arrived for me.
The message part said: "Cool it, Victor!"
The signature read: "Dr. Richter." ◆

Every time that lovers love
Venus watches from above;
Like a votive lamp within a niche,
She has every right to view
All the things that sweethearts do.
But heaven help us all if she should snitch. ◆

Once I went skiing on Thanksgiving Day
Down a slope in Vermont, it was snowing,
I made it to Montana by the seventeenth of May—
And if I hadn't hit that moose, I'd still be going. ◆

Said I, kneeling, as the Pope passed by:
"There, but for the grace of God, go I."◆

I think that I shall never see
My feet. ◆

A rose is a rose,
I suppose. ◆

My only aversion to vices
Are the prices.◆

Do you wanna be no one and just disappear
From this workaday whirl and strain?
Then hire my agent to guide your career
And you'll never be heard of again.◆

I love my little agents and my manager's a honey:
No matter where vacationing they always keep in touch.
My brokers both are jokers and at times
     they're even funny—
Never have so many done so little for so much. ◆

VICTOR BUONO, that delightful man in the large suit, with the expansive beard, deep voice, and exquisite diction, is, of course, *the* talented Victor Buono, actor (and Academy Award nominee), raconteur, lecturer—and now poet! Over and over again he has appeared on the major television talk shows, chatting, quipping *and* reading aloud his delightful verses. The response to his poetry has been enormous. The people want more . . . and more . . . and more. Mr. Buono is a native Californian (born in San Diego) and now lives in Van Nuys. He not only appears in plays and movies, but also lectures at clubs, colleges and universities throughout the country.